GOTCHA!

18 Amazing Ways to Freak Out Your Friends

Written by
David Acer

Illustrated by
Stephen MacEachern

KIDS CAN PRESS

Acknowledgments

This book is based on the television series *Mystery Hunters*, created by Jonathan Finkelstein. The series is produced by Apartment 11 Productions (www.apartment11.tv) in association with YTV and Discovery Networks International. Special thanks to Jonathan for making the book possible and to Mindy Laxer for making it happen.

Credits

p. 8: The ESP deck used in "Test Your ESP" was invented by Karl Zener in the 1930s.
p. 14: A magician named Ed Balducci published the first description of the "floating" trick described in "I Believe I Can Fly" sometime around July of 1974. He also said he learned it from his cousin years before, but the actual inventor is unknown.
p. 22: "Teleport Me" is a way to present a classic stage illusion created by U.F. Grant called "The Victory Girl Production."
p. 40: Making someone pick a card you want is called a "card force," and the card force used in "Time Travel" was invented by Max Holden.
p. 48: The Disappearing Dave trick in "Doubting Dave's Last Word" is called a "geometric vanish," and it's based on a version by Pat Lyons known as "The Vanishing Leprechaun."

Kids Can Press acknowledges the financial support of the Government of Ontario, through the Ontario Media Development Corporation's Ontario Book Initiative; the Ontario Arts Council; the Canada Council for the Arts; and the Government of Canada, through the BPIDP, for our publishing activity.

Published in Canada by
Kids Can Press Ltd.
29 Birch Avenue
Toronto, ON M4V 1E2

Published in the U.S. by
Kids Can Press Ltd.
2250 Military Road
Tonawanda, NY 14150

www.kidscanpress.com

Edited by Valerie Wyatt
Designed by Julia Naimska
Printed and bound in Singapore

The paper used to print this book was produced with elemental chlorine-free pulp, harvested from managed sustainable forests.

The hardcover edition of this book is smyth sewn casebound.
The paperback edition of this book is limp sewn with a drawn-on cover.

CM 08 0 9 8 7 6 5 4 3 2 1
CM PA 08 0 9 8 7 6 5 4 3 2 1

Library and Archives Canada Cataloguing in Publication

Acer, David
   Mystery hunters : gotcha! : 18 amazing ways to freak out
your friends / by David Acer ; illustrated by Stephen MacEachern.

Interest age level: Ages 8–12.
ISBN 978-1-55453-194-3 (bound). ISBN 978-1-55453-195-0 (pbk.)

1. Impostors and imposture—Juvenile literature. 2. Curiosities and wonders—Juvenile literature. 3. Occultism—Juvenile literature. I. MacEachern, Stephen II. Title.

BF1042.A34 2008   j001.9'5   C2007-906554-6

Kids Can Press is a *Corus*™ Entertainment company

Contents

Meet Doubting Dave

DAVE

Have you ever caught a ghost? Traveled through time? Predicted the future? Bent spoons with your mind? World famous Mystery Hunter Doubting Dave has, and now you can, too! But who exactly is Doubting Dave, and how does he do all this cool stuff? We tracked him to his lair (okay, kitchen) and asked him to tell us his secrets.

Q: Doubting Dave, who are you, and how do you do all this cool stuff?

Doubting Dave: I'm an alien superhero from another dimension, and I have many powers, including mind reading, teleporting and turning sock puppets into real people.

Q: Really?

Doubting Dave: Yes. Except for everything after "I'm."

Q: I see …

Doubting Dave: I'm actually a magician, scientist and skeptic, and I'm part of a team called the Mystery Hunters.

Q: Who are the Mystery Hunters?

Doubting Dave: We're three people who look for unexplained mysteries around the world.

Q: Like what?

Doubting Dave: Lake monsters, haunted houses, shoe salesmen who can fly … the usual.

Q: You actually met a shoe salesman who can fly?

Doubting Dave: Well, it turned out he was lying.

Q: I'm not surprised.

Doubting Dave: He wasn't really a shoe salesman.

CHRISTINA

ARAYA

Q: Wow! And who are the other Mystery Hunters?

Doubting Dave: Two very smart, very brave teenagers named Araya and Christina.

Q: What kind of mysteries have they hunted?

Doubting Dave: They've searched the skies, the forests and the oceans for proof of aliens. They've snuck into castles, graveyards and caves looking for ghosts. They've trekked through jungles, across deserts and down into sewers to hunt for monsters. And along the way they've run into all sorts of people who claim to be psychics, witches, mind readers, spoon benders, ghost channelers, time travelers and one guy who could turn his eyelids inside out.

Q: Gross.

Doubting Dave: Yeah. That one stayed with me.

Q: So what are people going to learn when they read this book?

Doubting Dave: How to teleport their friends, catch aliens on film, float off the ground — stuff like that.

Q: For real?

Doubting Dave: Do crocodiles burp?

Q: I don't know.

Doubting Dave: Me, neither. To answer your other question, you'll have to read on.

BURP!

Hypnotize This!

Do you want to put people under your spell using hypnosis? YOU CAN DO IT! With seven years of university classes and a license to practice psychiatry. Until then, here's a cool way to make it look like you're hypnotizing someone — try it on yourself right now. (You can do it while you're holding this book.)

1. Stand next to a wall like you're an open door, with the right side of your right foot up against the baseboard. Both feet should be under your shoulders and don't lean on the wall.

2. Slowly try to lift your left foot and step forward. Go ahead, I'll wait …

Back already? Couldn't do it, huh? That's because, to lift your left foot, you have to shift your weight to your right foot, but the wall is in the way.

6

3. When you try it on a friend, pretend to hypnotize her, then tell her what to do and watch her struggle. To "break the spell," snap your fingers and say, "Your strength is baaaaaaaack … NOW!" Then ask her to walk toward you. She'll have to turn away from the wall to do it, so she won't have any trouble.

Christina Gets Hypnotized

Can someone use hypnosis to make you do things you don't want to do, like eat worms or steal money or eat worms while you're stealing money? That's what Christina wanted to find out when she went to meet hypnotist Jeff Oatman.

him! She jumped up and started singing "Oops! … I Did It Again."

Jeff put her in a trance, then told her she was Britney Spears. Surprisingly, she believed

But was she really hypnotized? Here's what Christina said: "I could see myself doing it, but I didn't care. He didn't make me do anything I didn't want to do." So even when you're hypnotized, you're not really under anyone's control — unless Christina was hypnotized to say that …

Test Your ESP

Can you feel when someone is staring at you? Do you know who's calling when the phone rings? How many fingers am I holding up? If you answered yes, yes and three, you might have something called ESP! Here's a test to find out for sure. Try it with your friends and see who scores best.

What You Need:

- a piece of paper
- a pen
- an ESP deck (That's a deck made up of 25 cards, but with only 5 different symbols — a square, a circle, a plus sign, a star and 3 wavy lines. You can make your own ESP deck by cutting a big piece of cardboard into 25 equal squares, then drawing each symbol on 5 different squares.)

1. Shuffle the cards, then put them symbol-side down in a pile on the table.

2. Pick up the first card without looking at it and try to guess what the symbol is.

3. Write your guess on a piece of paper, then place the card symbol-side down beside the deck. Do this with the rest of the cards, writing your guesses in order and putting each card you've already guessed on top of the last.

4. When you're finished, turn the deck over. You should be looking at the first card you guessed. Compare it with the first guess on your paper. If they match, give yourself a check mark.

5. Compare the rest of the cards with the rest of your guesses, then count the check marks to see how many you got right.

How Did You Score?

1 to 5 guesses right:	Totally unlucky and definitely not ESP
6 to 9 guesses right:	Pretty lucky but probably not ESP
10 or more guesses right:	Congratulations! You may have ESP!

So does ESP really exist? I knew you were going to ask that. The truth is, nobody knows for sure. But one thing we do know is that most people who say they have ESP just make it look that way by using tricks.

The Midas Touch

How cool would it be if you could turn anything you touched into gold? Surprisingly, not so cool, at least according to King Midas. Legend has it a god gave him the golden touch (we never heard much about his brother, who apparently received the asparagus touch). But when Midas discovered he couldn't touch anything without it becoming gold, he realized his gift was a curse. He would have been better off learning this cool trick that makes it *look* like you can turn things into gold.

What You Need:

◇ 2 pencils the same size, one painted gold (use gold paint or nail polish) and the other a different color, such as red or blue
◇ a cloth napkin that's too thick to see through

1. Start with the gold pencil hidden under the napkin, like this.

Gold pencil

Corner should point toward you

2. Put the other pencil on the napkin like this.

Leave a gap between the corners

3. Tell everyone you're going to turn the pencil into gold, then pick up the corner of the napkin that's closest to you and fold it like this.

4. Slip your thumbs under both pencils and start rolling the napkin back toward you until the two corners are on top.

5. Here's the sneaky part. Roll the napkin just a tiny bit farther so that one corner rolls under and pops up around the other side.

6. Grab the corner that's pointing to your friend with one hand and the other corner with your other hand. Slowly pull the corners apart, revealing the gold pencil, which is now on top of the napkin. The other pencil will stay hidden underneath the napkin.

7. Hand out the gold pencil to distract (or "misdirect") your audience, then pick up the napkin with the other pencil underneath it and stick them both in your pocket.

Will anyone ever figure out a real way to turn things into gold? Here's an answer you probably weren't expecting — lettuce puppy. See? Very unexpected. But the real answer is, scientists have already figured out a way to turn something into gold — lead! They've done it in a big machine called a nuclear reactor. But the problem is turning lead into gold costs waaaaaay more than the value of the gold you make. As the chief scientist said when he got the bill — major bummer.

11

Make Your Own Bigfoot Prints

Do you want to start a Bigfoot legend near you? All you need is a big foot! Here's a way to make one that will leave massive footprints anywhere that's muddy.

What You Need:
- aluminum foil
- masking tape

1. Crumple lots of foil into five toes, a sole and a heel for your giant foot. The tighter you crumple the foil, the better.

2. Tape the pieces together, then wrap more tape tightly around the foot.

3. Tape the foot to the bottom of your shoe by wrapping tape around them both.

4. Push your foot down in a muddy spot, then lift it out. BEHOLD — a footprint that would fool Bigfoot's mother!

Araya and Christina Go Bigfoot Hunting

Could the world be full of Bigfoots? (Bigfeet?) Araya and Christina went looking for three different kinds — the Northwestern Sasquatch, the Florida Skunk Ape and the Louisiana Swamp Monster.

In Oregon, they tried attracting the Sasquatch with a recording of what researchers think is an actual Bigfoot cry.

In Florida, they tried luring the Skunk Ape into view with what locals say is his favorite food — apples!

And in Louisiana, Bigfoot hunters gave Araya a plaster cast from a swamp monster footprint that was three times bigger than his own foot!

But in the end, Araya and Christina never saw any of the hairy palookas. Does that mean they don't exist? Yeeeeeennnnnnnnnnnnnnmm mmmmmmmmmmmmuuuhhhhh … It's hard to say. But unless we find proof other than just footprints (like hair, or bones, or giant toenail clippers), the most anyone will ever be able to say is that their feet exist.

I Believe I Can Fly

Here's a cool trick that makes it look like you can float off the ground just by thinking it. (If nothing else, it's a fun way to pick low-hanging apples.) You'll need a friend to help you practice. And it *does* take practice, but it's worth it.

1. Stand in front of your friend (facing away from her) and take three big steps forward. Turn a little to your left.

2. Put your feet together so they're touching along the insides. The front (toe end) of your right shoe should be hidden from your friend.

3. Spread your arms to help you keep your balance. Keep your left foot flat and lift it up as you lift your right heel.

Your heels should still be touching so your friend can't see between them. Since the toe end of your right shoe is hidden from your friend, she'll see both feet rising off the ground.

4. Let your feet drop back down to the ground and bend your knees a little when you land, like you've just jumped from a swing. If your friend says she can see how you're doing it, try turning a little more or a little less to the left before you lift off. You can also try moving a little farther away or a little closer.

So can anyone float off the ground for real? YES! People in hot-air balloons. Other than that, we're all pretty much stuck down here with the squirrels.

Test Your House for Ghosts

Are you alone? Are you sure? Maybe there's a ghost in your room right now! Here are two easy tricks ghost hunters use to find ghosts. All you need is a compass, a thermometer and, if you're lucky, a ghost! But do they really exist? Absolutely! I've seen lots of compasses and thermometers …

What You Need:

◇ a digital thermometer
◇ a compass that tells directions

1. Take your thermometer and compass to the creepiest room in your house (like the attic or basement). Hold one in each hand and move around the room. Check along the walls and behind anything where a ghost might be hiding.

2. Ghost hunters say that ghosts are cold, so if you find a spot in the room where your thermometer suddenly drops, that could be a ghost! They also say that ghosts are electromagnetic, so if the needle on your compass starts wavering, that could be a ghost too.

What should you do if you think you've found a ghost? You should remember two things:

A cold spot can be LOTS of things other than a ghost. Sometimes cold air sneaks in from vents, holes or cracks in the walls. So if you find a cold spot, look for a natural cause before you conclude that it's supernatural.

A compass can be very sensitive, and it doesn't take much to affect one. Magnets (even hidden ones) and lots of electrical appliances can do it. So check for non-ghostly causes before you blame a ghost.

Do ghosts exist? Seriously — I'm asking you. Because right now, your opinion is as good as anybody's. Lots of people say they've seen, heard or felt ghosts (I even have a friend who says he can smell them), but that's not proof — that's a reason to look for proof.

17

Spoon Bending

Here's a fun way to make it look like you're bending a spoon when you're not. It's an illusion that freaks out everyone who sees it (especially spoon collectors).

1. Stand the spoon on a table and wrap both hands around the handle like this.

2. Secretly move your left pinky behind the spoon handle like this.

4. From the front, it looks like the spoon is bending in half! Wait a second, then hand out the spoon to show it was all a hoax.

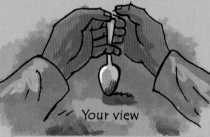

Your view

3. Gently lower your hands straight down to the table as if they're still holding the handle, but actually let the spoon lean back toward you.

Audience view

Still your view

18

Araya Goes to Spoon-Bending School

If an owl showed up at your home with an invitation to a spoon-bending school, would you go? Araya did. Except instead of an owl with an invitation, he got an e-mail with an attachment. When he arrived at the school, he saw more kids and LOTS of spoons that they had supposedly bent with the powers of their minds.

Araya and the other kids were each given their own unbent spoons, and by the end of the class, those spoons were bent, too!

So did Araya and his classmates really bend their spoons with powers of their minds? Yeeeeeeee eeeeno … They actually bent them with their hands.

But the teacher distracted them by saying things like, "The molecules in the spoon will do what you want," and, "Imagine the spoon getting soft." So when they were done, even *they* weren't sure how the spoons got bent.

Make a Fake UFO Photo

Have you ever seen a UFO? Of course you haven't. Nobody has, because UFOs don't exist. Even the word UFO doesn't exist. And I'm not just saying that because there are two men in black suits standing behind me. But if there aren't any UFOs (which there aren't), how could people have photographs of them (which they don't)? The answer is simple — people take pictures of things they *think* are UFOs, then these things turn out to be normal, everyday objects, like airplanes, weather balloons or even just birds. So there you have it — problem solved. There's no such thing as UFOs. Glad I could help. Now let's talk about something that does exist — being a patriotic citizen. Patriotism is very important, because y...

Whew! Okay, they're gone. Now I can show you a way to make fake UFO photos that look so real, you might get a visit from the Men in Black yourself!

What You Need:

◇ a piece of tape
◇ a silver coin
◇ a car
◇ a camera

1. Make a small loop of tape and stick it on the back of your coin.

2. Tape the coin a little more than halfway up the windshield of the car.

3. Get in the back seat and point your camera at the windshield. Make sure the coin is in frame, then focus on the horizon and start snapping photos.

4. In the photos, the coin will look like a flying saucer hovering near your car!

Has anyone ever taken a picture of a real UFO? Well, now that the Men in Black are gone, I can finally tell you the truth — I don't know. And (more truth) no one else knows, either. Why? Because every UFO photo that's ever been taken is either blurry or suspicious or clearly a hoax. Does that mean they're all fakes? No. But it would take an alien to figure out if any of them are real, and by then, what's the point?

Teleport Me

Wouldn't it be great if you could disappear from one place and reappear in another? No more taking the bus to school. No more lining up at airports. No more getting trapped in your grandmother's hugs. Impossible? Maybe. But here's a fun way to make it look like you can do it.

What You Need:

◇ 2 cardboard boxes with their tops and bottoms cut out
◇ 2 friends

One box big enough for a friend to fit in. Cut a hole in one side that your friend can crawl through.

A slightly bigger box that will fit over the smaller one

1. Before your audience arrives, flatten the bigger box and hold it like this, with one of your friends crouched behind it.

2. When it's showtime, have your other friend (or "assistant") lift up the smaller box to show that it's empty. (Make sure the hole in the side faces away from the audience.)

3. Your assistant puts his box down like this. Then your crouching friend secretly crawls into your assistant's box through the hole.

4. Pick up the flat box and say, "This is a teleportation machine." Open it and, with your assistant's help, slide it over the other box.

5. Give the boxes one complete turn so your audience sees all sides.

6. As you pretend to push a button on the box, say, "I just press a button and watch what happens." Then your crouching friend stands up like she appeared from nowhere.

So can anyone really teleport things? Well, in 2002, scientists made a beam of light teleport from one end of their lab to the other. Of course, as amazing as that is, it's not nearly as impressive as teleporting a person. But it does mean that, one day, teleporting might be possible (although probably not in time for you to get out of your grandmother's next hug).

Everybody Loves Ouija

Can a ghost answer questions through something called a Ouija board? Great question! Let's make a Ouija board and ask a ghost!

What You Need:

- a cardboard rectangle about the size of a place mat
- a black marker
- a smaller piece of cardboard shaped like a large teardrop with a big hole in the fat end and felt (or something smooth) on the bottom

1. Write the alphabet in two rows across the top of the board. Along the bottom, write Yes, No and Good-bye.

ABCDEFGHIJKLMN
OPQRSTUVWXYZ

Yes   No   Good-bye

2. Put your pointer (the teardrop-shaped cardboard) in the middle of the Ouija board. Now rest your fingertips lightly on the pointer. You can also do this with friends.

3. Start by asking a simple question, like, "Is there a ghost here?" Sit quietly and wait, but don't push or pull the pointer. Some people believe that ghosts will guide the pointer to answer your question. For this question, they would probably move it down to the word YES.

4. If you get an answer to your first question, ask some more, like "What is your name?" or "Why are you here?" The ghost should answer each question (usually pretty slowly) by making the pointer slide around on the board, pointing to letters and spelling out words.

So let's say the pointer moves — does that mean there are ghosts in your room? IT CERTAINLY DOES ... not mean that. What's actually happening is that you're moving the piece yourself. Your muscles spasm without you even realizing it, which starts the pointer sliding. Then you begin to guess ahead and form words. Don't believe me? Put on a blindfold, then ask the Ouija board another question and have a friend who isn't blindfolded write down the letters you point to. Chances are you'll end up with total gibberish.

Make Your Own Lake Monster Video

Sixty-five million years ago, the oceans were full of giant sea monsters. Could some of them still be hanging around in lakes? That's a question everybody wants answered (especially sushi chefs). Here's your chance to show the world you've actually found one! (A sea monster, not a sushi chef.)

What You Need:

◊ a video camera
◊ a lake
◊ a friend
◊ a homemade lake monster
(Use your imagination and make it any way you want. Here's how I made my first lake monster: I started with a pool noodle that was about half as long as my arm. Then I untwisted a metal coat hanger and ran it up through the middle of the pool noodle. I bent the pool noodle into the shape of a giant serpent sticking its head out of the water, then I wrapped some gray cloth around it. Finally, I attached my lake monster to a flat piece of wood using more wire and gave it eyes, creating this terrifying beast!)

Okay, it may not look all

that terrifying up close, but yours doesn't have to either. You can make it look real and (if you want) scary on video by using these four simple tricks.

1. Something videotaped from far away can look mysterious …

… even when it's not. So try videotaping your lake monster from as far away as possible.

2. You can't tell how big something is if there's nothing near it to compare it to.

So if you want people to think your lake monster is BIG, don't show anything other than water around it, and make sure nothing floats by that gives away its real size.

3. Just because something's moving ...

... doesn't mean it's moving on its own. So attach some fishing line to it and have a friend pull it through the water.

4. Finally, move the camera a lot and make the focus blurry like this.

That's how most "real" lake-monster videos look, which makes them hard to prove or disprove — because you can't really tell what you're seeing.

Araya and Christina Go Fishing for Lake Monsters

Araya and Christina always wanted to see a lake monster (they're a little nutty), so they packed up their swimsuits and went to two of the most famous "monster" lakes in the world.

Araya tried to find "Nessie" in Scotland's Loch Ness using sonar.

And Christina tried to catch Alaska's Lake Iliamna monster with a homemade fishing lure.

Did either of them end up getting their monster? Would you be surprised if I said YES? Me too, because the answer is no. Araya actually found out that Loch Ness doesn't have enough food in it for a lake monster to survive. Most of the sightings there are probably logs that float up from the bottom of the lake.

But Christina discovered that there might be giant sturgeon in Lake Iliamna, and they sometimes get big enough to look like lake monsters.

Nobody's ever caught a giant sturgeon there, but Christina left her lure in the lake, just in case …

Move Things with Your Mind

Can you turn this page just by thinking about it? Try it now ... WAIT! Don't forget to come back if it works! Okay, go ahead ...

It's harder than it looks, isn't it? But don't feel badly — this page is pretty big. Here's a way to do it with a smaller piece of paper that works every time.

What You Need:

◇ a pencil
◇ a ruler
◇ a piece of paper about 10 cm x 10 cm (4 in. x 4 in.)
◇ a cork
◇ a sewing needle

1. Use your pencil and ruler to draw a line from each corner to the opposite corner. You'll end up with a big X.

2. Bend any two opposite corners of the paper, one corner up, the other corner down.

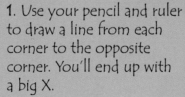

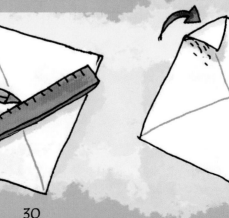

30

3. Stand the cork on a table and carefully stick the needle into it. Balance the paper on the needle by putting the center of the X on the end of the needle.

4. Cup one of your hands and hold it near the paper. Make it look like you're concentrating. Nothing will happen at first, but if you wait a few seconds, the paper should start to spin, sometimes slowly, sometimes quickly.

Why? Heat from your hand causes tiny air currents that push the bent corners of the paper, making it move. But since no one can see the air currents, it looks like you're moving the paper with your mind.

So can anyone really move things with their minds? Yes — YOU! When you pick something up with your hand, you're moving it with your mind, because your mind is moving your hand. Other than that, our minds are pretty much only good for doing stuff inside our heads, not outside.

Zombie Dinner Guest

The next time you have friends over for dinner, why not introduce them to your headless zombie cousin? He makes a lot of noise banging his cutlery on the table, but on the plus side, you'll never catch him wearing one of your hats.

What You Need:

◦ a friend wearing a big shirt that buttons down the front

1. Have your friend sit on the far side of your dining room table. The top two or three buttons of his shirt should be undone.

2. Tell him to tilt his head forward, then you pull his collar back behind his neck and do up the top button.

3. Ask him to put his head under the edge of the table so it can't be seen. Now straighten out his collar and make sure it's right up against the table.

4. Give him a knife and fork to hold on the table and tell him to bang them down like he's hungry. From the other side of the table, he looks like a headless zombie demanding food.

Can dead people really climb out of their graves and walk around as zombies? I traveled all the way to the Royal Cemetery in England and tracked down chief grave digger Albert Vernon to ask him that very question. Here's what he said — "No." And there you have it! Zombies may be common on TV and in the movies, but in the real world, the only dead things walking around are people who stay up all night worrying about zombies.

Psychic Healing

Have you ever tried healing a cut or a bruise or even a pus-filled pimple just by touching it? (Well, okay, I guess that's how everyone heals a pus-filled pimple.) If you did, and it didn't, try this fun way to make it look like you have healing powers.

What You Need:

- a hankie or napkin with a hem around the edges that's like a little tunnel on all four sides
- 2 toothpicks

1. Before you do this trick, secretly slip one toothpick into the hem of the hankie so it's near a corner.

2. Tell a friend how you once found a bird with a broken wing. Say that you picked it up and your hands got warm, then it flapped its wings and flew away! That's when you realized you had the power to heal little things like birdies ... (sniff). Now say that you can actually heal anything that's little, like a broken toothpick. To prove it, bring out the hankie and lay it on the table.

The hidden toothpick is at the upper right corner.

3. Put the second toothpick in the middle of the hankie.

4. Fold the upper right corner over the exposed toothpick.

5. Fold the other corners over the middle, then grab the part of the hankie with the *hidden* toothpick, but don't lift it.

6. Tell your friend to hold this toothpick with both hands. When he has it, you let go. He'll think it's the toothpick he saw because he doesn't know there's a *hidden* toothpick. Now tell him to break the toothpick.

7. Once he's broken it, ask him to let go. Tell him you'll use your special healing powers to mend the toothpick. Wave your hand over the hankie, then unfold it to reveal the whole, unbroken toothpick. The broken toothpick will stay hidden in the hem.

Can anyone really heal people just by touching them? Maybe if they touch them with ointment. Other than that, nobody has ever proven they have magical healing powers — just medical ones.

Make Your Own UFO Video

What would your family say if you showed them a video of a UFO you taped through your window? First it hovered in the sky for a few seconds, then it flew away and disappeared behind something big, like a building, or a mountain, or one of those Marmaduke dogs.

They'd probably say the same thing everyone says when they see this incredible hoax: What the heck is that?!? It's actually a fake UFO video you can make without leaving your house, and it's so convincing, videos just like it have been posted all over the Internet as the real deal!

What You Need:

- a video camera
- a tripod
- a piece of cardboard that's about the same shape as something tall you see out your window. (If it's a building, just use a cardboard rectangle. If it's a tree or something else, cut out a similar shape.)
- a flashlight
- a friend who's in on the hoax

cardboard

cardboard

1. When it's dark out, put your video camera on a tripod and point it at the window. Turn out the room lights and turn on the camera.

2. Have your friend hold up the cardboard shape behind the camera, then stand behind him and shine your flashlight on the window.

3. Through the camera, the light will look like a UFO that has just flown into view outside your window.

4. Move the flashlight back and forth in a swooping motion across the window like it's a UFO flying around. Make sure the light doesn't hit the cardboard (yet).

5. Now here's the cool part. Zip the light over so that it's suddenly blocked by the cardboard.

The light on the window will disappear as if it flew behind the object outside!

Is every UFO video just a hoax like this one? Not necessarily. Lots of people have filmed things in the sky that look like spaceships. But they could also be seagulls or airplanes or the helium balloon I accidentally let go of when I was six. In other words, so far, all these videos really prove is that video cameras exist.

Araya Goes to NASA

Did astronauts on a mission to the moon accidentally catch a UFO on film? Araya went to NASA to find out. Amazingly, when he got there, they told him they *did* film a UFO, then they let him take the film out of their vault!

But was this really an alien spaceship? And did NASA try to cover it up? No and no. In 2004, scientists used brand new, high-tech equipment to analyze the film and figured out that the UFO was actually just a lamp sticking out from Apollo 16.

Even more amazingly, when Araya watched it, he saw exactly what they said was there. In 1972, something that looked like a UFO flew right past Apollo 16 while it was on its way from the moon back to Earth.

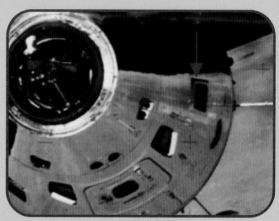

It looks like the only secret NASA might have been covering up was their favorite brand of light bulb.

Time Travel

Do you want to be the first kid on your block who can travel through time? Here's a cool card trick that makes it look like you can!

What You Need:

- a deck of cards with a big black X drawn on the face of every card except the four of clubs (ask permission to do this)
- a watch

1. Start with the unmarked four of clubs on top of the deck. You're the only one who knows it's there. Put your deck on a table with the back facing up. Ask a friend to cut the deck near the middle and put the top half beside the bottom half.

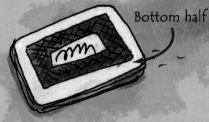

Top half with four of clubs on top

Bottom half

2. Say, "That's perfect. I'm going to mark where you cut." Pick up the bottom half and put it crosswise on the top half.

3. Say, "You cut the deck anywhere you wanted, right?" This gets your friend's attention off the deck for a moment so she won't remember which half is which. Now lift the top half of the deck and set the first card of the bottom half to one side, face down. Say, "This is the card you cut to." It's actually the card that was on top of the deck when she cut, but she won't notice because you distracted her.

Four of clubs

Remove this card

4. Put the deck back together, but leave the single card where it is. Tell your friend you're going to go forward in time and look at this card. Pretend to press a button on your watch, then say, "I'm back, and I saw what the card is — it's the four of clubs." When your friend turns the single card over, she'll see the four of clubs.

5. Say, "But that's not all! After I went forward, I went BACK in time and put a mark on all the cards I knew you wouldn't cut to." Ask your friend to look through the rest of the deck and she'll see a big X on every card.

Is time travel possible? Many scientists believe it is, and not just mad scientists — regular scientists with assistants who weren't made from spare body parts. That means NOT being able to travel through time may someday be a thing of the past.

You don't have to believe in ghosts to catch one on film. In fact, most so-called ghost photos are just accidents (the happy-coincidence kind, not the poop-in-your-pants kind). Here's a way to snap a picture of a ghost yourself by making one of those accidents happen on purpose.

Make Fake Ghost Photos

What You Need:
◇ a small mirror
◇ a camera

2. Put the mirror on (or in) whatever you're taking a picture of, then stand back and snap some flash photos.

1. Find something spooky to take a picture of, like a tombstone or a dead tree or even just a dark corner in your basement.

3. If the angle is right, the flash will hit the mirror, then bounce back to your camera, making a burst of light that can look very ghostly.

Christina Snaps a Photo of a Ghost

Would you walk into a cave that's supposed to be haunted? Christina did. Except she wasn't just there to see a ghost — she wanted to catch one on film!

But what kind of ghost haunts a cave? Ghosts of bats? Spiders? Mold? Well, legend has it this cave in Kentucky is haunted by the ghosts of people — LOTS of people. Could the ball of light in this photo Christina took be one of them?

Christina showed me the photo and found out that a ball of light is usually just the camera flash reflecting off something shiny or even off dust in the air.

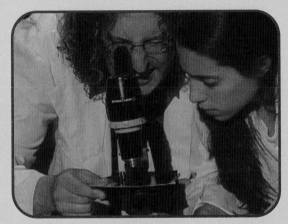

That's when Christina realized there were lots of people in the cave who had equipment and tools that could have reflected her flash back at her. There was also lots of dust. So chances are the light in her photo was just a reflection. OR A DEADLY GHOST-BAT LUNGING AT HER FACE! ... But probably just a reflection.

Who Wants to Be a Mind Reader?

Do you think it's possible to read minds? What if I told you I'm receiving your answer right now? You'd probably think I was faking it, and you can fake it, too, with this sneaky trick that makes it look like you're a mind reader.

What You Need:

- a mug
- 4 different coins, like a penny, a nickel, a dime and a quarter
- a secret assistant who's in on the trick

1. Put the mug and four coins on the table.

2. Turn your back to the table and ask someone (NOT your secret assistant) to pick up any three coins and put them in a pocket. Now, with your back still turned, ask your secret assistant to turn the mug upside down and cover the remaining coin. As he does this, he's going to tell you which coin is under it without saying a word. How? Just imagine the mug is a clock and the handle is the hour hand. Your assistant turns the handle to tell you what the coin is.

For a penny, 12 o'clock

For a nickel, 3 o'clock

For a dime, 6 o'clock

For a quarter, 9 o'clock

3. When you turn around, your assistant will have put the mug in one of the four positions above. All you have to do is check the handle, then close your eyes and pretend to be mind reading while you tell your friend which coin is under the mug.

Lots of people say they can read minds, but can anyone actually do it? I'm thinking the answer right now (it rhymes with "snow").

Make a Crop Circle

Your neighbors will think aliens have landed! Your newspaper will take photos! The evening news might even ask you for an interview! Who made the mysterious crop circle that appeared in a field near your house? Was it aliens? Ghosts? A cow with an inner-ear infection? The world will forever wonder! (But you'll know the truth.)

What You Need:

- a field with tall grass (Make sure you ask permission to use it.)
- a wooden stake with a big spool of string tied to it
- a board with a piece of rope attached to each end

1. Stick your stake in the field (you did ask permission, didn't you?), then stretch out the string in any direction as far as you want your crop circle to go. Keep the string taut as you walk around the stake, stomping down the outline of your circle. From here on, you won't need the string and stake.

2. Put the board down at the edge of the circle and pick up the ropes. Step on the board with one foot, flattening the grass under it.

3. Lift the board by its ropes and keep stepping on it as you walk around in smaller circles. When you get to the middle, you've made a crop circle!

Araya's Crop-Circle Hoax

Araya went to the place where crop circles started — England — and tried a little crop circle hoax of his own. After dark, he snuck into a field with some crop-circle artists and stomped out a simple design using boards.

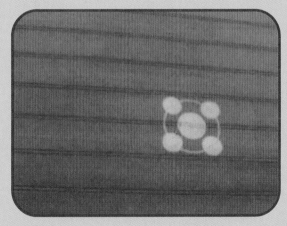

The next morning, he went up in an airplane to see how it looked. He could hardly believe his eyes.

It looked just like the crop circles supposedly made by aliens! In fact, it turns out that any crop circle (even the complicated ones) can be made by people. Of course, if there are alien spaceships orbiting Earth, they could probably make crop circles from up there too, using lasers or microwaves or a board with reeeeeally long ropes. The question is, why would they?

Doubting Dave's Last Word

So now that you've learned every trick, hoax and experiment in this book, are you ready to be a Mystery Hunter? Almost! There's just one more thing you need to know, and it's something most of us learned the hard way. (I learned it while stuck in quicksand and being pooed on by a bear). Even when you think you're seeing a ghost or hearing a psychic or smelling a zombie, try to remember — things aren't always what they seem.

The ghost might be an optical illusion, the psychic is probably faking it, and the zombie could just be a rotting dead guy who escaped from his grave ... WAIT, NO! ... Okay, well, I guess it's good to keep an open mind.

Anyway, the point is, it's up to *you* to dig deeper, look for clues and talk to experts. And you can start right now by trying to figure out how I disappear into thin air! Just photocopy this page and cut out the boxes below, then follow the instructions to see me vanish. But don't get discouraged if you can't solve the mystery. At least you're not stuck in quicksand and being pooed on by a bear.

Arrange the three pieces like this and count the Doubting Daves. There should be 15.

Now arrange the pieces like this and count again. Only 14, right? DOUBTING DAVE #15, WHEEEEEEERE AAAAAARE YOOOUUU ...?